CONTENTS

Copyright   1

Equinelightenment   5

Acknowledgements   6

Introduction   7

A Beginner's Mind   12

Joy   19

Mindfulness in Action   26

Clear Awareness   34

The True Nature of REality   44

Energy   52

Equanimity   59

Tranquility and Serenity   67

Conclusion   73

About The Author   77

EQUINELIGHTENMENT
Discover the Buddha in your Barn

Michelle Hefner, ACC
Zen H Coaching
Cover Art by Maria Dalbaeva

ACKNOWLEDGEMENTS

Special thanks to my husband Edwin Reed for his love, support, and encouragement. His wonderful sense of humor keeps me inspired. His intelligence, honesty and gentle critiques were invaluable in the writing of this book. Thank you for being the love of my life.

To all of the horses who have guided me down amazing paths. Thank you for sharing your ancient wisdom. Learning to listen to you has profoundly impacted my life. You asked me to give you a voice and I've made it my mission to do so by teaching people the art of listening with the heart.

INTRODUCTION

My teacher arrives through the mist, he floats to me un-
heard, unseen, his presence not sensed until his breath
tickles the back of my neck. He invites me to join him
in the fullness of the present moment, the world of the
senses. "What do you feel when you hear the birds' songs?"
He asks. " What do you see with the eyes of your heart?
Who are you without your stories?" His questions stir in
me a forgotten memory of the body's intelligence, igniting
my heart's wisdom. His teachings are as profound as those
of the most enlightened Zen master's. His patience with
my ignorance is without comparison. He is always truth-
ful with a forgiving heart. He models equanimity perfectly
as I strive to get there. He makes me acutely aware of the
interconnectedness of all and the ease of communication
beyond words. He is my Buddha, he is my horse. And then
he snorts a big, sloppy, snotty exhale onto my clean, white
tee shirt.

Lessons

1. Choices have consequences
2. Don't sweat the small stuff

The amazing experiences I've witnessed as an equine assisted coach have expanded my perception of horses as
master teachers beyond measure. Inspired by their profound wisdom, I wanted to share their teachings not only
with my coaching clients but with the whole of the eques-
trian community. Focusing on what horses most want us
to learn, lessons that align perfectly with the 7 aesthetic

principles of Zen Buddhism, I called my workshop, Equine-lightenment: Discover the Buddha in your Barn. This book was inspired by the stories from workshop experiences. I've presented them here as one journey for Katie and her horse, Joe. Each chapter begins with their story and is followed by a Zen koan, further explaining the principle. Finally, I've included activities from my workshop that help your horse guide you on your path to mental clarity, peace and enlightenment.

Your Buddha in the Barn

Horses embody a pure Buddha nature, the foundation of all wisdom. Because they possess no egotistic attitudes, they represent the highest enlightened mental state. Their innate essence is perfectly suited to reflect, non-judgmentally, how we are progressing on the journey to discover our own Buddha nature. Their acute perception makes them highly attuned, sentient beings who clearly and honestly illuminate the path when we have strayed. Like giant compasses that show heart and harmony as due North, they patiently, and sometimes not so patiently, steer the needle back to heart whenever our distractions take us off course. They skillfully jolt us out of old patterns of thinking, allowing new perspectives to break through. All of this they express through their unique, wordless language, one we can only hear when listening with our hearts. They are the ultimate teachers of Zen.

Why Zen, why now?

In today's chaotic world, people are turning to contemplative practices like Zen in search of peace. They are awakening to the awareness that the fruitless drive to satisfy cravings is leaving them empty, causing them stress and making them ill. Too many people identify with the rider in the following koan:

> A horse suddenly came galloping down the road. It seemed as if the man had somewhere important to go. Another man, who was standing alongside the road shouted, 'Where are you going?' and the man on the horse replied, 'I don't know! Ask the horse!"

Zen is experiential in nature, the goal being to bypass the intellectual and emotional mind in order to access our own inner wisdom or Buddha essence. Our horses model pure Buddha nature. By engaging in intentional, interactive encounters with our teachers, we can access the many gifts of Zen. Through the activities in this book, you will begin to experience a more peaceful mind, increased focus and self awareness, greater trust in your own intuition and a profound feeling of connection with your horse and the world around you.

Koans in Zen

Koans are riddles or stories used to unravel the greater truths about oneself and the world. They are parables presented by Zen teachers to evoke something deep in the listener. The answer is not, "...achieved by looking out of the corner of your eye to see if everybody else is getting the same results as you or by trying to find out what others have already discovered. It is achieved by going down into one's own inner, secret place and asking there for a direct encounter with the world, independent of convention. "-- Alan Watts.

On a daily basis, our horses assign koans to us. They keep us in the question of a story like an explorer in a foreign land, learning a new language, forced to lift veils of perception so we may see more clearly what is. The riddles your horse presents to you are handily solved through the application of the aesthetic principles of Zen Buddhism.

The 7 Aesthetic Principles of Zen

Every interaction with your horse is an invitation to practice the aesthetic principles of Zen. These principles are the roadmap to the conscious cultivation of deeper connections to ourselves and others. They comprise the contemplative foundation needed to take back the reins of our lives to live in equanimity, harmony and peace.

Equinelightenment turns your barn into a sacred temple and allows your horse to become your personal Buddha. Embarking on this journey, you and your horse will gain a deeper understanding of each other, greater clarity in communication and a newfound depth of mutual love and respect. You may want to keep a dedicated journal for all of the remarkable experiences you are about to have with your horse as you:

- Enhance your creativity and problem solving by seeing through the lens of a beginner's mind
- Gain powerful insights through mindfulness
- Practice equanimity, the space of wisdom, freedom, compassion and love
- Cultivate peace through clear awareness
- Develop your intuition and expand your awareness through exploring the true nature of reality
- Deepen mutual trust through the intentional experience of elevated emotions
- Stretch your ability to feel the presence and intention of another sentient being and communicate beyond words, using your body as an energetic sensory device.
- Strengthen the bond with your horse through tranquility

My soul honors your soul.

I honor the place in you where the entire universe resides.

I honor the light, love, truth, beauty and peace within you,

Because it is also within me.

In sharing these things we are united, we are the same, we are one.

A BEGINNER'S MIND

Chapter 1

"The mind of the beginner is empty, free of the habits of the expert, ready to accept, to doubt, and open to all possibilities." --Shunryu Suzuki

Katie and Joe

"I was reminded of who I was as a child, my true essence before everyone in my life began molding me into the person they wanted me to be. Seeing through a child's eyes, I was instantly transported to a place of expansiveness, curiosity and compassion." --Katie

On an autumn night, at a barn surrounded by sumptuous nature, I met Katie and her imposing, beautiful bay thoroughbred, Joe. It was the first night of my workshop, a time to get to know the participants and to learn a bit about their relationships with their horses.

Katie adored her horse. But he did not seem to return the sentiment. He was difficult to catch so she had resorted to tricks aimed at preventing him from running away whenever she carried a halter into the pasture. She went so far as to hide the halter under her shirt and bribe him with treats. Once caught, Joe did not like being groomed. He was always moving away, restlessly, from the brushes. His attitude had turned surly over time and he sometimes nipped while being led.

As Katie spoke, I sensed a low buzz coming from her. Her tall frame held the intensity of a rubber band stretched to its limit. She was on the precipice of crying, trying hard not to fall. A stifled yawn was filling my chest as her intensity siphoned energy away from me. Horses have taught me to use my body as a sensory device, perceiving like they do through the senses. As the tempo of her speech accelerated, my breathing became more shallow in response. I intentionally inhaled deeply, imagining that I was sending calm towards her through my heart with each exhale. The tension of holding back the tears dissipated and she allowed them to flow. The release was visceral. The buzz disappeared. Katie's shoulders hunched, her head bowed as if she wanted to hide the fact that she was crying. Sandra, the barn owner, reached for Katie's hand and gently squeezed it.

After regaining her composure, she shared a few biographical facts. Katie has a successful chiropractic practice, she is recently divorced and she lost her mother, following a long illness, at the beginning of the year. The upheaval in the past year and a half of her life, has left her feeling like she's on a rollercoaster without breaks. Six months into the amusement park ride, she bought Joe as a way to make time for herself. Riding had been her passion from childhood into her twenties, when the busy flow of life swept her away from the one thing that gave her the greatest joy. Since buying Joe, she goes to the barn after working 14 hour days to spend time with him, grabbing a bite to eat on the way. She wanted him to be her "therapy". Over time, the more she needed him as her therapy, the less he wanted to be around her.

"Fortunately for us, horses can be very generous with do overs," I told Katie. After introductions, we went to a large arena, with the horses loose to wander around. There, the ladies spent time remembering who they were at 5. They all had common essences that were silly, fun, courageous, free and curious. The memories lightened the mood of the group. All thoughts of "problems" dissipated and the arena filled with laughter, as we remembered the inner child who is always present within us. The horses slowly drifted towards the group. Joe stayed a short distance away but was finding it difficult to resist the lighthearted energy. He hesitantly moved closer, watching.

The ladies continued the mood by grooming the horses with their non-dominant hands. They walked amongst the horses, grooming one and then another. A cacophony of laughter permeated the arena. Brushes were flying out of hands. Repeatedly, the dominant hand tried to grab for the brush. The experience of clumsiness was one that many had not experienced in a very long time. The horses were enjoying the grooming but, more importantly, they were enjoying the fun. Joe was now in the middle of the circle, his curiosity getting the best of him. He stood while Katie brushed him.

Zen Koan

Nan-in, a Japanese master, received a University professor who came to learn about Zen. Nan-in served tea. He poured his visitor's cup until it was full and then kept filling. The professor watched the overflow until he could no longer restrain himself. "It is overfull. No more will go in!"

"Like this cup," Nan-in said, "you are full of your own opinions and speculations. How can I show you Zen unless you first empty your cup?"

Lessons

1. "In the beginner's mind there are many possibilities, in the expert's mind there are few."-- Shunryu Suzuki.

In a paper by Professor Victor Ottati from Loyola University in Chicago, which appeared in <u>The Journal of Experimental Psychology</u> in November 2015, his findings showed that "self-perceptions of expertise increased close-minded cognition." Horses, if given a choice, will always move away from a closed or cluttered mind. I've never met a horse, however, who was not drawn to a curious, open hearted presence, the foundation of a Beginner's Mind. They seek our essence, the person we are without the stories. By remaining in the present moment, we can experience life as if all were new, free of preconceived judgements (the past) and liberated from concerns for what has not yet happened (the future). To approach experiences as if, at any moment, we will be granted a mystical secret, quiets the mind. Through a curious, alert presence we can meet horses where they live and hear the inner voice of intuition.

Lessons

1. "Treat every moment as your last. It is not preparation for something else."-Shunryu Suzuki

2. "Quiet the mind and the soul will speak."-- Majaya Sati Bhagavati

Benefits of a Beginner's Mind:

1. Expand your perspective
2. Become open to new ideas and possibilities
3. Reduce worry and anxiety
4. Find creative solutions to life's challenges

Activities

1. Who were you at the age of 5?

One way to get a glimpse into the beginner's mind is to remember who you were at the age of 5. At this age, most of us had no worries. We had not yet become self-conscious. We lived life in a world of unknowns and we were comfortable playing there. Everything was new and interesting. Next, remember how the adults in your life attempted to mold you into who they thought you should be. To do this, simply bring to mind all of the ways they corrected you. Perhaps you were too loud, too quiet, too gregarious, too shy, too active... Who were you before being molded? This is who your horse sees and who they want to be with.

2. Take time to open your heart each morning

Standing near your horses, imagine sinking down into your heart space. Breathe into and out of your heart. Allow your heart to open and bloom. Bring to mind all you are grateful for. Hold that thought until you feel a physical sensation. Notice your horse's response.

3. Groom with your non-dominant hand

Take a brush with you to the pasture. Before approaching your horse, open your heart by admiring your horse. Next, approach your horse and groom him with your non-dominant hand. Doing this often generates lots of giggles. Experiencing what it is like to be clumsy again is a great way to practice a Beginner's Mind.

4. Ask a question you think you know the answer to

Use the spirit of enquiry to question your own perspectives and beliefs concerning your horse.

5. Eliminate the word "should"

Spend a day noticing how often you think or say the words should or shouldn't.
Each time you notice it, attempt to reframe your experience from a different
perspective.

6. Experience the moment fully

Describe the background of what you see, bringing curiosity to the context of your experience. Imagine experiencing each of your senses as your horse experiences his. How does this enrich the moment for you?

7. Photograph your pasture

Capture new insights into your horse's life by taking photos of the pasture and your horse from unusual perspectives. Discover new flowers, bugs, plants you've never noticed before. Stay open and alert for the mystical secrets waiting to be told to you.

JOY

Chapter II

"Sometimes your joy is the source of your smile, but sometimes your smile can be the source of your joy."--Nhat Hanh

Katie and Joe
"Through this experience, I was able to move from a place of separation, fear and hesitancy to one of implicit trust, deep connection and true joy."--Katie

We started the morning with the horses loose in the large arena. We were seated in a circle in the arena and the horses were wandering amongst us. All except for Joe who was at the far end watching the goings on. I told Katie to just enjoy the activities with the other horses, that it was up to Joe to decide whether he wanted to participate. To set the mood, we took time to share sensory experiences with the horses. The ladies allowed the horses to smell different essential oils, determining their favorites. Following the oils, the group piqued the horses' interest by playing a variety of musical instruments. With our attention focused on bongo drums, a loud clanging noise drew our attention to the picnic table. There, a lovely buckskin mare named Daisy had decided to play the singing bowl. With the stick held between her teeth, she beat it loudly against the bowl. She appeared very proud of herself as we doubled over in laughter. We continued with the sense of touch, exploring where each horse preferred to be scratched. Joe's curiosity had led him to the group. Katie discovered that he loved having his belly scratched best, showing his appreciation by stretching his neck out long and puckering his lips. After enjoying the shared sensory experiences, we returned to the circle to practice invoking elevated emotions at will.

Cultivating elevated emotions with intention sets us up for success with our horses. We can choose the information we want to transmit through the hearts' electromagnetic field. The heart field is a communication highway that carries the frequencies of all of our thoughts and feelings. Horses respond, react to and reflect the energy that is transmitted through these fields. A herd of horses share their very large heart fields, moving into and out of one another's spaces, in constant communication. Attunement to the herd members' psychophysiological states creates cohesion amongst the horses and serves to keep them safe. When we understand that our every thought creates a biological response (psychophysiological state), we gain powerful insights into how our horses' behaviors are reflections of what we are feeling moment to moment.

Katie's life had been tumultuous in the past year and a half. She had become aware of how her stress caused Joe's negative behavior but did not know how to change it. His increasingly volatile reactions to her caused her to fear him which, in turn, caused him to react, creating a vicious cycle. One way we can begin to shift dynamics is to learn how to intentionally summon elevated emotions.

The group of women stood, eyes closed as I led them through a body scan. The scan brings about a shift from the Beta brain waves, that chatty, monkey mind, to the relaxed, present moment awareness of the Alpha waves. First the women imagined they were breathing deeply into and out of their hearts, allowing their hearts to fill the chest cavity. As they continued the breath, the horses drifted back to the group, meandering into the center of the circle. Even Joe. The women became exquisitely aware of each of their senses, one at a time. Next, they remembered an event in their past that had brought them great joy. They stayed in that event, carefully recalling every aspect of it, all the while breathing deeply. The horses began licking, chewing, yawning and rolling their eyes back in their heads. Joe started flapping his lips while exhaling. I suggested to the women they could send the frequency of joy out through their fields like ripples across water, towards the horses. Joe made his way to Katie and stood facing her, his head lowered in relaxation. When the women slowly opened their eyes, Katie found Joe inches from her. He exhaled again, a big sloppy one, spraying her face and chest with snot. Her heart exploded with happiness and tears ran down her cheeks. She felt that he had finally chosen to be with her instead of rejecting her.

She and Joe stood together, bathing in joy. The suspicious horse I had met the night before had transformed into the picture of contentment. Katie's energy, too, had shifted from a low, depressed state into one of contentment. To build trust with Joe, however, she would have to show up in a similar way for him repeatedly so he could begin to trust her to provide a safe field of connection.

Lessons

1. "When a person projects a heart coherent field filled with caring, love and attention, living organisms respond to the information in the field by becoming more responsive,

open, affectionate, animated and closely connected."--Stephen Harrod Buhner, The Secret Teachings of Plants.

Zen Koan

A king told the sage that he was ready to do anything in order to be happy. The sage asked, "Are you sure you are willing to make any sacrifice in order to obtain happiness?" The king replied that, for happiness, he was ready to make any sacrifice.

The sage explained happiness is not in possessions. The king would have to give up all of his wealth to attain joy. The desperate king gathered all of his valuables-gold, silver, jewels, put them in a large sack and brought the sack to the sage. The king asked what he should do next. The sage told him to close his eyes for one minute. The king obeyed. With the king's eyes closed, the sage picked up the sack and started running.

When the king realized what had happened, his unhappiness turned to anger. The sage had cheated him! The king chased him through the narrow alleys and all around the town. When the king finally caught the sage, he said, "You're no sage, you're a charlatan! You just wanted to rob me. The sage said, "Don't you see it? I just gave you the formula for joy. Only an hour ago you had all of your wealth. But you were unhappy. Then I took all of your valuables away from you. Now you have them back and you are happy! Where did the happiness come from? From the wealth? Or did it come from inside of you?

The king bowed at the sage's feet and thanked him for the

lesson.

Lessons

> 1. "Happiness is a choice, not a result. Nothing will make you happy until you choose to be happy...Your happiness will not come to you. It can only come from you."--Buddha

In our horse's mind, we can never be too joyful. The more joy you experience, the deeper connection you will have with your horse. An open heart is a communication highway that allows you to hear your horse's voice and allows him to hear your clear intentions. Learning to intentionally generate joy at least once a day will improve your overall health, enhance all of your relationships, prevent depression and set the mood for the day. It can be as simple as remembering a particularly joyful moment in your life.

Fortunately, our subconscious minds are not capable of distinguishing between an event that is actually happening now and one that we are simply recalling in our mind's eye. The body responds in the same way by flooding it with feel good, health inducing hormones. When you practice summoning higher level emotions like joy, gratitude, abundance, peace, love, awe or amusement, your horse will gravitate towards you. No more walking out in the pasture to fetch him. Your elevated emotion will act as an irresistible magnet.

Benefits of Joy and other Elevated Emotions:
1. Boost your immune system
2. Fight stress and pain
3. Increase resilience

4. Gain strength and energy
5. Experience deeper connection

Activities

1. The Body Scan

A body scan is one of the most efficient pathways to mindfulness. The purpose is to tune into and focus on the sensations of the body and to become aware of the sensory experiences in the moment, noticing the sensations through the lens of curiosity rather than judgement. A scan increases your ability to focus and takes your emotional temperature. It relaxes the mind from the busy Beta brainwaves into the present moment Alpha waves, where our horses live when awake and comfortable. When we access Alpha waves, we meet our horses where they are. When you first begin, you may find it easier to listen to a guided body scan. There are many available online.

- Begin by standing or sitting with your eyes closed.
- Take deep, slow breaths, filling your lungs and belly before exhaling.
- Feel the weight of your body.
- It might be helpful to imagine a beam of colored light entering through the top of your head, flowing down your face and neck before it continues to each area of the body.
- Move your attention slowly through the body. Stop for a few seconds at each body part and notice how it feels. Is it tense? Relaxed? Painful? Neutral?
- When your attention wanders, simply

notice that and return to the body
- Notice any quirky thing that comes to mind as you proceed. The body speaks more as an artist than a scientist.

2. Share sensory experiences with your horse

In Zen, there are 6 worlds-the seeing world, the hearing world, the smelling world, the tasting world, the touching world and the intuitive world. Using a collection of essential oils, notice the subtle ways your horse shows preferences. Collect a range of small musical instruments. Notice which sounds your horse enjoys. Allow him to explore them as well. Next, find which brush your horse prefers. Note how he responds to each one, again paying close attention to the different physical signs that express his preferences.

3. Invite your horse to play

The spirit of play is a curious, open heart, an intention of carefree fun with no other agenda but joy. Join your horse in the arena with toys, props, anything that might spark your horse's curiosity. Joy is contagious so, as long as you are having fun, your horse will want to join in.

4. Choreograph a dance

Play your favorite song. Design a dance for you and your horse. It might include backing 3 steps, turning right then left, shoulder in, stepping under with a hind foot... the possibilities are as limitless as your imagination. After choreographing your steps, play your song in the arena and partner with your horse in a beautiful dance.

MINDFULNESS IN ACTION
Chapter III

"We are what we think. All that we are arises with our thoughts. With our thoughts, we make the world."--Buddha

Katie and Joe

"I became aware of the negative thoughts and anxiety I had around my relationship with Joe. When these shifted, he showed me the connection he really desired and he also showed me a side of him I had not met before. It felt like he offered and I accepted very deep healing on many levels." -- Katie

In the next activity, the women planned a fun, interactive activity with their horses. The intention was to experience, in real time, how their thoughts create their realities. It gave them an opportunity to practice mindfulness, including heightened emotional awareness, presence and interconnectedness.

The women were encouraged to use any of the props laying around (pool noodles, balls, stuffed toys), music, treats, whatever their imaginations could conjure. The most important part of the planning, though, was for them to decide ahead of time which emotions they wanted to experience and how they wanted their horses to feel. For example, a participant might want to feel amused and have her horse feel curious. Next, the women spent some time visualizing the interaction, experiencing the elevated emotion they wanted before the event took place. Katie wanted to "dance" with Joe, combining joy and a sense of abandon. She wanted her horse to experience curiosity and connection.

She went into the large arena with Joe and queued a song from her playlist. She started to dance.

'Friday night and the lights are low, looking out for a place to go...' Katie swung her arms, she twirled in a circle, half heartedly.

'...where they play the right music, getting in the swing, you came to look for a king...' Katie's king ignored her.

She raised her arms above her head, twisting her hands to the beat of the song. She approached him, begging him to join her. He blinked his giant eyes then walked over to his pasture mate.

Katie stopped dancing and stood without moving, looking at the ground for a long while. She later confided that, while standing there, her mind filled with thoughts of judgement, separation and despair. Perhaps it was ridiculous to expect him to dance with her, she thought. After what felt like an eternity, she began again as she recalled that her intention for the dance was to experience joy and abandon. Eyes closed, she visualized what that would look like for her and conjured into her being the emotions she wanted to feel.

'...Dancing Queen, feel the beat from the tambourine, oh yeah..'

Something about her dance had shifted. She tossed her head, twirling her brown pony tail, arms flailing, opening her body, her heart to the rhythm of the song.

'...everything is fine, you're in the mood for a dance...' She stomped her feet, swiveled her hips.

'...and when you get the chance, you are the Dancing Queen...'

The energy transformed into a mesmerizing ecstatic dance, the music moving Katie freely wherever the rhythm took her. It was as if she were in a trance. As we watched, the contagion was palpable, compelling our bodies to involuntarily rock back and forth to the beat.

Now Joe's curiosity was piqued. He hesitantly started towards her. He stopped and glanced back at the group with an expression that said, "has she lost her mind?" Then, drawn by the magnetism, he continued towards her.

'...looking out for another, anyone will do, you're in the mood for a dance, and when you get the chance, you are the Dancing Queen...'

When her arms went high in the air, Joe raised his head. When she lowered to the ground, bending at the waist, he lowered his nose to meet her. She danced towards him and he backed away, turning and running a circle around her but returning again to face her. She aimed her dance at his shoulder and he stepped away to the side in perfect step with her lead.

'...you can dance, you can jive, having the time of your life, ooh, see that girl, watch that scene, digging the Dancing Queen..'

They continued dancing as partners until the song came to an end. Kate dropped to the ground, exhausted, laughing like a crazy woman. Joe came to her, his breath on the back of her neck, flapping his lips.

She returned to the group, thrilled, breathing heavily from the dance. I asked her what had shifted. She said, in the beginning, she felt she needed to perform but she felt limited because Joe was ignoring her. The stories had started in her mind, "He doesn't like me, he doesn't trust me, he doesn't want to be with me…" Then, when she remembered her intention, she shifted her mindset to match what her heart wanted. Once she opened her heart and started enjoying herself, Joe responded to who she was being and what she was doing, compelling him to join in. She did not have to coax or cajole him. She felt like they were creating together, in collaboration with a connection she had not felt before. Most importantly, she and Joe had fun together!

Then we went to lunch, hearts full of laughter and joy… With Dancing Queen stuck in our heads!

Lessons
1. "Life is a dance. Mindfulness is witnessing that dance."--Amit Ray
2. "Mindfulness is a way of befriending ourselves and our experience."--Jon Kabbat-Zinn

Zen Koan
Two men visit a Zen master. The first man says: "I'm thinking of moving to this town. What's it like?"
The Zen master asks: "What was your old town like?"
The first man responds: "It was dreadful. Everyone was hateful. I hated it."

The Zen master says: "This town is very much the same. I don't think you should move here."
The first man leaves and the second man comes in.
The second man says: "I'm thinking of moving to this town. What's it like?"
The Zen master asks: "What was your old town like?"
The second man responds: "It was wonderful. Everyone was friendly and I was happy. Just interested in a change now."
The Zen master says: "This town is very much the same. I think you will like it here."

Lessons

1. "Once you realize that all comes from within, that the world in which you live is not projected onto you but by you, your fear comes to an end."--Nisargadatta Maharaj
2. "We do not see things as they are, we see things as we are."--Talmudic saying

Mindfulness is the human ability to be fully present, aware of our surroundings and our interactions without being overwhelmed by what is happening. It is the ability to intensely experience all you are sensing and feeling in the moment, free from judgement. Training your brain to quiet into mindful presence is a practice that actually changes the structure of the brain. Mindfulness leads to emotional awareness, interconnectedness and it brings to light how our thoughts create our reality. It is the path that leads us out of the sympathetic nervous system (stress) and into the parasympathetic nervous system (peace).

The sympathetic nervous system, wherein lies the fight

or flight response, is an important gift. It ignites whenever there is immediate danger. When activated, stress hormones of adrenaline and cortisol flood our bodies, giving us "superhuman" strength and speed, if necessary. Our bodies do not know the difference between a real threat and daily stress, though. They are not designed to live in a constant state of danger. Continuous presence of these hormones eventually lead to a cascade of negative effects. High blood pressure, heart disease, diabetes, breathing problems are all results of our bodies' prolonged stress response. The chain reactions emanating from the sympathetic nervous system do not go unnoticed by our horses. As prey animals, they recognize these as the physical signs of a predator about to attack.

Through mindfulness, we can choose to switch on the parasympathetic nervous system, the portal to interconnectedness. Mindfulness permits us to become present, aware and in heart coherence, allowing our horses to connect with us on ever deeper levels. Mindful presence is the single greatest gift you can give your horse and all of your loved ones. It expands our conscious awareness, allowing us to become more sensitive to both our internal and external lives while increasing appreciation for each moment. Watch your horses begin yawning, licking, chewing, rolling their eyes back in their heads or doing full body shakes while you practice mindfulness in their presence.

Lessons
1. "Nothing can harm you as much as your own thoughts unguarded."--Buddha
2. "With our thoughts we make the world."--Buddha

Benefits of Mindfulness:
1. Cultivate a heightened awareness of reality
2. Create a new reality by changing your thoughts
3. Experience peace and interconnectedness
4. Nurture your intuition

Activities

1. Create your reality with intention

To create the reality you want, begin by setting an intention before an interaction with your horse. Decide ahead of time what the purpose of the activity is. Visualize the experience. List all of the emotions you would like both you and your horse to experience and know what end results you would like. Notice in what ways your experience differs from your normal interactions.

2. Interconnectedness--Lean on me

In this activity, you will apply meta awareness to 2 experiences. First, find something solid to lean your back against. Rest there and notice what information you get from it. What does it feel like? What is it's temperature? Does it feel sturdy? Does it make a sound? Do you feel supported? How does it smell? Imagine how it would taste. Next, smell it. What does it smell like? Touch it with your fingertips. Describe it's texture. What do you feel inside your body as you lean against it? What thoughts float through your head?

Next, lean against your horse at his or her shoulder. Consider the same questions as above. Notice what stories your brain wants to make. If your horse walks away from you, what emotions come up and where do you feel them in your body? Describe, without emotion, judgement or inference, how he responds to you. How does the sense of connection differ between the inanimate object and your horse? Rate the level of trust you experience on a scale of 1-10. What are your takeaways from this activity?

3. **Meditate with your horse**
    Buddha was asked, "What have you gained from meditation?" "Nothing! However, let me tell you what I have lost: Anger, Anxiety, Depression, Insecurity, Fear of old age and death."
    There are many guided meditations available on the internet. Phone in hand, sit on a mounting block and quietly meditate. While doing this, don't be surprised if your horses lay down near you, stand with their noses over your head or partake in other fascinating behaviors.

4. **Investigate an emotional experience**
    In your journal, write a description of the last time you had an emotional experience with your horse (good or bad) Name the emotion. What precipitated the onset of the emotion? Where did you feel it in your body? In what ways was your horse "mirroring" the energy of the emotion you felt?

CLEAR AWARENESS
Chaper IV

"The greatest wisdom is seeing through appearance."--Buddha

Katie and Joe
"It was such an epiphany to learn that I am responsible for all of my interactions. I can set an intention for every experience and make it a reality." --Katie

After lunch, I explained the concept of clear awareness to the group. Katie asked if this could be a reason for Joe often dancing around her and not respecting her boundaries. "Yes," I responded," when we don't know what we want, when our heads are full of confusion, we cannot be a leader. For insecure horses, it is frightening to be tethered to a ship lost in a storm!" With the women having just experienced how their thoughts create their realities, (Katie dancing to connection with Joe), they could see how a scattered mind would result in a fractious horse. Practicing meta awareness teaches you to become aware of what you are experiencing in your body and your mind, and with our horses reflecting that experience in their behavior, we can begin listening to them to know what our inner state is moment by moment.

To practice clear (meta) awareness, the group would participate in an activity diving into the 4 elements of the human experience-observing, thinking, feeling and wanting. The arena was divided into four quadrants. When it was Katie's turn, I led her through a body scan, bringing her back into the present moment. As was typical, before beginning, Joe was as far from us as he could be. Once Katie became present, Joe was drawn to her. With him at her side, she attached the lead line to his halter.

Katie wanted to focus on her relationship with Joe. She led him to the area of Feeling, where she wanted to begin. I asked her to become aware of the emotions arising in her as Joe practically trotted in place next to her. Noticing where she experienced the emotions in her body, her face scrunched, her eyes closed and she said she felt a tightening in her solar plexus and in her gut. She said she felt distant from him and she was suddenly disappointed after the gains they had made in the morning. Joe stood next to her but was looking at the group, pulling slightly, wanting to leave Katie's side. We let Joe decide which section to go to next. He led her to Wanting.

I asked her, "What do you want at this moment?" Eyes closed, she breathed into her heart and said, "Confidence in myself". I told her to imagine what Confidence would look like and to sculpt her body into a form that represented confidence for her. She grew a few inches, straightening her back, raising her chin, setting her jaw. With this, Joe, standing beside her, raised his head and looked sideways at her. His brow was furrowed in curiosity. Maintaining this stature, she led Joe to the Thinking quadrant. His demeanor had shifted to a more calm, respectful one as he walked attentively next to her.

When Joe started to lag behind, head butting her in her lower back, moving her along, I asked, "What thoughts are coming up for you?" "Sometimes I doubt that I know what I am doing with him. Maybe buying him was a mistake.

He was supposed to be my therapy and now he just seems like a stressful problem I don't have an answer to." "Who would you be without these thoughts?" I asked. Her head was down. She made designs in the sand with her boot. "I would be a blank slate of possibility." He brought his attention back to her and nosed her in her heartspace. Returning to the Feeling section, I asked, "What does a blank slate of possibility feel like in your body?" "Expansive, really. Like a burden is off my chest." she responded. Joe licked and chewed and shook his head hard. As she said this, her posture had straightened again, her chest opened and her energy rose. Joe mimicked her stance, raising his head and somehow becoming taller and broader. Maintaining this energy, they walked to Observing.

"What do you see from this perspective?" I asked. "I see that I am responsible for all of my interactions with Joe, that for him to feel secure with me, I have to be confident and clear with my intentions and actions. I also see what a burden it must have been for him when I expected him to be my 'therapy' " she said. "How will you express confidence and clarity? What will that look like?" I asked. "Before interacting with him, while I'm still in my car, I'm going to visualize what I want to do with him, set an intention for the results I want and notice what emotions are stirring in me so I can acknowledge them and try not to bring them to Joe for him to fix. Then, I am going to shape my body into confidence and notice what that feels like before going into the barn."

She took the confident energy and her plans back to Thinking. I asked if her perception had shifted in any way. She said what came up for her was that Joe had not signed up to be her therapist. It was too large of a burden she had placed on him. She had not taken his needs into account. What he needed was the comfort of a confident leader who was present and connected rather than lost in her monkey mind, constantly worrying and doubting herself. Joe responded with more licking and chewing and yawning, as if he knew she had finally gotten what he had been trying to tell her for so long.

Lessons

1. The result of not seeing the world clearly is suffering.
2. When we practice clear awareness, we become more attentive, aware and alive to others.

Zen Koan

"Once there was a young warrior. Her teacher told her that she had to do battle with fear. She didn't want to do that. It seemed too aggressive; it was scary; it seemed unfriendly. But the teacher said she had to do it and gave her the instructions for the battle. The day arrived. The student warrior stood on one side, and fear stood on the other. The warrior was feeling very small, and fear was looking big and wrathful. They both had their weapons. The young warrior roused herself and went toward fear, prostrated three times, and asked, "May I have permission to go into battle with you?" Fear said, "Thank you for showing me so much respect that you ask permission." Then the young warrior said, "How can I defeat you?" Fear replied, "My weapons are that I talk fast, and I get very close to your face. Then you get completely unnerved, and you do whatever I say. If you don't do what I tell you, I have no power. You can listen to me, and you can have respect for me. You can even be convinced by me. But if you don't do what

I say, I have no power." In that way, the student warrior learned how to defeat fear."--Pema Chodron

Lessons

1. "Sometimes the mind is like a wild horse. It doesn't know how to behave. If emotions and passions are not controlled, how can you have stillness?"--Master Choa Kok Sui

2. "The mountains that you are carrying, you were only supposed to climb."-Najwa Zebian

Clear awareness makes you the alert, wise witness to your life. As the observer, you learn to respond to situations rather than react, recognize emotions for the messages they deliver and then release that energy. Clear awareness is taking a pause to consider whether your next action is in the best interest of all involved. It is seeing events as they unfold, free of emotional reactions that stem from the shadows of previous experiences and free of judgement. It is learning to differentiate the external circumstances from your internal emotional experience of them.

Horses model clear awareness. The herd has no time for doubt, indecision, skepticism or vacillation when a hungry mountain lion is headed their way. There will be neither discussion nor argument over the next steps to take. As one, they will turn to gallop away, manes flowing in the wind until they reach safety. When the danger has passed, they will release the emotion of the moment with full body shakes and yawns before returning to grazing.

To exercise the clarity muscle, begin with introspection. Become aware of your perceptions and how they are driven by the emotions of past experiences. Then ask yourself if they are true. Begin to notice, too, when you are projecting your own emotions and thoughts onto another. When you feel triggered, take the time to mindfully explore all of the feelings that arise from it before acting. You will begin to embody the knowledge that you are not your thoughts and emotions but the one who is experiencing them. With this realization, you are free to choose your appropriate responses, notice the patterns in your life and clearly communicate your heart's desire.

Lessons
1. When we are not clear on what we want, it results in confusion for our horses.
2. Connection combined with clear awareness is the formula for success in all relationships.

Benefits of Clear Awareness
1. Heighten your awareness, without judgement, of what you are sensing and feeling.
2. Observe your thoughts and patterns, noticing the ones that cause fear, guilt, shame or any other negative, limiting beliefs.
3. Increase empathy for yourself and others.
4. Gain clarity in your goals, communication and visions.
5. Discover hidden strengths that were buried in confusion.

Activities
1. Clean language
To begin practicing clear awareness, in your journal, describe an event using "clean language". That is, include only what IS, free of all judgement and perception, a reality that every person, of every background and culture can agree upon. Next,

include in your description your own behavior, thoughts and body language. Narrate it from the viewpoint of your horse. The challenge is to differentiate between your thoughts and what is simply happening externally, in the moment. It can be fun as you begin to see yourself and the environment from your horse's perspective.

2. The 4 intuitive senses

In this activity, you will become aware of and cultivate your 4 intuitive senses.

Discover which one is an innate strength for you and which ones need practice. Focus on each sense with your horse present, as your intuitive guide. Notice his response as you experience each one. Your horse might touch a part of your body with his nose, lick, chew, yawn or shake. Which intuitive sense is the strongest for you? Which one is weakest? Notice if you have a block.

- **Intuitive Knowing**--People who are strong in this sense experience instantaneous knowing. They trust their 1st impressions. To practice this sense, think of a question you need an answer to and look upward, focusing on the crown of the head. What is the first answer that pops into your mind?

- **Intuitive Feeling**--For those gifted in intuitive feeling, their bodies are like antennas. Their gut feelings are instant. They have the ability to sense negative energy in a room. Focusing on the solar plexus, breathe into and out of that area and ask your question. The body speaks more as an artist than a scientist so don't be surprised if the answer comes in the form of a color, poem or a strange, long forgotten memory.

- **Intuitive Hearing**--If words, music or sounds speak to you suddenly, your strength is in intuitive hearing. To practice this sense, focus on the point above the ears, the temporal lobe. As you focus your attention there, notice changes in what you hear. See if you can feel a vibration when you focus on this area. Ask your question and notice what you hear.

- **Intuitive Vision**--People who are strong in intuitive vision will not make a decision until they have visualized all of the options. They may also be able to see auras around people and animals. You can connect with your horse by focusing on your third eye with a soft focus. Ask your question and see what appears in your mind's eye.

3. The 4 Elements of the Human Experience

Invite your horse to join you on a journey through the 4 elements of the human experience, paying close attention to where he tells you to go and what his opinion is. Create 4 quadrants, one for each element. Walk from one to another with your current challenge in mind.

- **Observing**--Practice paying close attention to the environment, the background that is the context for your life. Take a photo of this context. Looking at it, note your response to the picture. Describe the external world you see in the photo. Next, consider a challenge in your life. Imagine what it would look like in a snapshot. What is the context? What is your internal response to it?

- **Thinking**--Considering your challenge, what assumptions are you making around the subject? Ask yourself what perceptions you are bringing to the situation? What assumptions are you making?

- **Feeling**--Differentiate between the emotions the challenge brings up for you and the feelings you experience. Feelings are sensations in the body and emotions are energy in motion that cause happiness, sadness, worry, etc. Name the emotions you feel and explore how each one feels in your body.

- **Wanting**--What is the particular outcome you desire? In our society, we often communicate in the language of complaint. Focus solely on what you do want from the challenge, not on what you don't want.

4. Energetic Connection

- Begin this activity by sharing space with your horse without an agenda. With your eyes closed, inhale deeply for a count of 4. Hold the breath for a count of 4. Exhale to the count of 4 and then wait another 4 seconds before inhaling again. Repeat this five times. Next, imagine sinking down into your body and feeling it from the inside out. Connect with each of your senses before opening your eyes.

• Walk with your horses, matching their energy. What is it like to feel connected at a distance? Notice when the horses walk away or disconnect from you in distraction. What shifted in you energetically that caused the disconnection? What is your emotional response to their actions? What does it feel like in your body? Bring their attention back to you by walking away, hiding or otherwise piquing their curiosity. Begin again to mirror their energy, moving into and out of their space. Play with the energy of connection and notice how your feelings change over the course of your experience.

THE TRUE NATURE OF REALITY
Chapter V

"Your true nature cannot be avoided, just as a tree cannot deny its own roots."--Zen Thinking

Katie and Joe

"This afternoon, I learned to know Joe as he is instead of as a projection of my emotional state and as he is when he is not reflecting my own energy. It turns out that he is not the stories I made up for him"--Katie

Katie had divined many stories about Joe. He was aloof, easily distracted, distrustful, suspicious, nervous, lacking in focus. "He must have been abused in the past and he became aggressive as a result" was one of her favorites. Convenient though it was, that story did not exactly align with the horse he was when she first got him. He was once well mannered. It was only over time that he had become dangerous, uncontrollable and scary in Katie's experience. To discover who he was, we needed to unpack which traits were hers' and which were his.

The owner of the barn, Sandra, had a different experience of Joe. She felt he was a model citizen in her day to day interactions with him. So, who was Joe? In groups, the ladies shared insights of their own positive and negative traits to begin distinguishing between who they are and who their horses are not. They listed the ways their horses frustrated them and considered the times in their lives they had frustrated those closest to them in similar ways. They analysed how their negative patterns played out in the relationships with their horses by exploring their emotionally driven perceptions and assumptions. Once they recognized their personal characteristics and responsibilities, they listed the many wonderful ways they describe their horses to others.

After this conversation, the women went to the arena to interact with a horse that was not their own. Their goal was to notice how the horse responded to their energy as they approached. After, they were free to groom the horse, lead him or just spend time with him/her. They took notes of their subjective experience, focusing only on what they were experiencing in the moment. Next, they noticed the objective experience, what every being was experiencing in the arena. Finally, they noted the intersubjective experience, what the person and horse were experiencing together.

Cassie (a boarder at the barn) interacted with Joe. As I watched, Joe sauntered straight to Cassie. As she took notes, he stood with her, lipping the pen. At one point he took the notepad out of her hand, raising it into the air, with papers flapping. Cassie laughed as she retook possession of the notepad. They continued to interact with an air of playfulness.

On the other side of the arena, Katie was struggling with a large, black warmblood named Marlene. The two of them were having a different kind of dance. When Katie reached a close proximity, Marlene began stepping away with each step Katie advanced towards her. After a while, Katie surrendered her goal of making a physical connection, sat on a mounting block and began journaling. Her eyes, though, continuously floated over to Joe and Cassie. Curiously,

Marlene chose not to leave. She stood nearby maintaining a 10 foot distance between them.

When we reconvened in the barn to share experiences, Katie admitted she felt a bit jealous of the seemingly effortless interaction she witnessed Cassie have with Joe. She confessed that her attention had been divided, her experience split between her own and Cassie's. She was watching who Joe was with another person and, at the same time, she felt rejected by Marlene. Marlene's owner, Norma, interjected, "But Marlene was there with you. She stayed, sharing space with you. You were not present for Marlene." It was then Katie realized that she was the one who tended to be 'aloof', not Joe. She confessed that, in general, she had a difficult time being in the present moment with her mind constantly judging, worrying, dreading. Why would anyone, let alone a horse, want to be in that energy? A look of epiphany came over her face. She said, "The many criticisms I've had of Joe are all critiques of myself. And I am a fierce judge of myself!"

"Watching Joe interact with Cassie," I asked Katie, "what did you learn of his true nature?" She took a deep breath. Her closed eyes searched the images playing across her memory. "I saw a horse who was mischievous, curious, silly. That's how I want him to be with me." Tears were streaming down her cheeks now." I asked, "Who do you have to be to connect with his essence?" "I need to be me without the stories, the stresses and worry. I need to be my 5 year old self, full of courage, fun and mischief. My true nature is joy, just as Joe's is."

Lessons

      1. Wisdom is knowing the nature of all things,

free from the distortions of the mind.
2. The way things are versus the ways in which we interpret them is unlocked through connection and contemplation.
3. When our reality is a form of projection, our perceptions mislead us into believing we are separate.

Zen Koan

An old man meditating by the riverside opened his eyes to see a scorpion flailing helplessly in the water. The water washed the scorpion nearer to a tree growing on the river bank. Supporting his body on one of the long roots stretching into the water, the old man extended his hand out to reach the creature. His fingers barely touched the scorpion when it stung him.

The old man instinctively withdrew his hand. A moment later, he got back his balance and again lay down on the roots to rescue the scorpion. This time the scorpion stung him well and truly. The old man lay there in agony, his hand bloodied and swollen.

A traveler who was passing by saw the whole incident happen. He shouted, What's wrong with you? Only a fool or madman would risk his life trying to save that evil, vicious creature! Do you realize you could have died trying to save that scorpion?

Still lying there, the old man turned his head to look at the traveler calmly. "Dear brother, it is the nature of the scorpion to sting. That does not mean I can change my nature, which is to save."

The scorpion behaved true to its nature. So did the old man.

Lessons

1. Seeing reality as it is is a prerequisite to well being and mental health.
2. "The ability to observe without evaluating is the highest form of intelligence."--Jiddu Krishnamurti

In Buddhism, much philosophical contemplation is focused on exploring the true nature of reality. It's a worthy pursuit considering most suffering derives from resisting what IS.
It is easier said than done, however, considering reality is often subjective, shaped by our perceptions, assumptions, expectations and mood in the moment.

Once you begin contemplating reality, things get fascinating. Look out your window. What do you see? How would you describe it? Would you imagine that everyone, looking at the same view, would have the same description? All that we experience is colored by a range of factors including our stories, our limiting beliefs, our insecurities, even how our morning has been. Through that window, I may perceive a beautiful, clear blue sky, imagine a soft breeze and relish the warmth of the day. For another person, however, that clear blue sky means there are no clouds to block the intense, hot sun. The heat feels oppressive and the breeze may feel like a furnace. The descriptions are both reality for each individual. Does a universal reality exist or only millions of perspectives?

Assumptions and expectations play a role in sculpting our

experience of reality as well. A person might assume that their stocky quarter horse is capable of performing high level dressage moves. Their expectations do not align with the true nature that hundreds of years of breeding has created. Over time, that quarter horse may suffer injuries due to being asked to perform skills for which his breeding did not prepare him. Resistance to the nature of the horse and the resulting illusion about the horse's capabilities will eventually cause frustration and disappointment.

Bring awareness to your stories, assumptions and perceptions to see the true nature that lies beneath it all. Many difficulties in life evaporate when we surrender into acceptance of what is.

Lessons

1. "Enlightenment is not about becoming more spiritual...It's about becoming aware of the true nature of reality."--Free Thinking Guru
2. "Those who forgive themselves, and are able to accept their true nature. They are the strong ones."--Masashi Kishimoto
3. "Losing an illusion makes you wiser than finding a truth."--Buddha.

Benefits of contemplating the true nature of reality

1. Maintain an open and curious mind.
2. Gain freedom from suffering.
3. Expand your awareness, understanding and compassion.

Activities

1. **Cultivate curiosity around your stories**
   - Make a list of the stories you have in your life. You can recognize your

stories by noticing whenever you say "I should...", whenever you make an excuse for why you cannot do something or whenever you mentally beat yourself up. Spend a day noticing any of these occurrences and write them in your journal.

- Next, make a list of the stories you have about your horse. These will include suppositions of what his/her life was like before he came to live with you, why he spooks at certain things, who he dislikes and/or why he cannot perform the way you think he should.

- For each of the stories, ask yourself this simple series of questions from Byron Katie's The Work:

  - Is it true?
  - Can you absolutely know it is true?
  - How do you react, what happens, when you believe that thought?
  - Who would you be without that thought?

Journal your answers and include any shifts in perspective that arise.

2. **Plan an experience with your horse.** (It can be as simple as leading him on a hike or having a grooming session.)

- Create an intention, decide on a purpose for the interaction and know what your desired result is. (incorporating clear awareness)

- Next, visualize it ahead of time (mindfulness)
- Decide how you will bring in joy (gratitude, curiosity of a beginner's mind) to achieve an open hearted connection
- Strive to see through his eyes. Take note of what he is experiencing subjectively, what is happening objectively and what the two of you are experiencing intersubjectively.

What new insights arise from this awareness? How did this intentional experience differ from previous ones? Apply these steps to an experience with a family member or friend. Notice the difference in the quality of your connection. Write your reflections in your journal.

3. Conscious leading

Lead your horse in full awareness and presence. Notice where and when each foot is moving. Decide how far away from you want your horse to be from you. Bring attention to each of your senses while walking. How do you empower your horse as you ask for turns? Try asking only when your horse is able, turning left when his left foot is coming off the ground. How does your body prepare for the turn? What is your response when your horse does not follow or gets distracted? How do you respond in life when there is no momentum for what you want? Notice if and when you disconnect from your intention. What is your horse's response to the disconnection? How is this experience a metaphor for your life experiences?

ENERGY
Chapter VI

"Everything is energy and that's all there is to it. Match the frequency of the reality you want and you cannot help but get that reality. There can be no other way. This is not philosophy. This is physics."--Bashar

Katie and Joe

"When my actions became congruent with my heart's desire, Joe began responding to who I was being and what I was doing. When I experienced a shift in my energy, that was the invitation for him to join me."

The next activity of the day involved the ladies having an experience with their horse that comes from the heart. The qualities of the heart are all associated with the elevated emotions of love, gratitude, innocence and authenticity. Free from the egoic filter, the heart is the voice of your highest self.

After a body scan, Katie began breathing deeply into and out of her heart. She then asked her heart what it wanted to do with Joe at this moment. When she received her message, she turned and entered the round pen with him. She stood for a long time in the center. Joe wandered around, curious about those of us sitting outside of the arena. I noticed a shift in Joe's energy as he turned his attention to Katie. He walked over to her then and positioned his body so that his heart was in line with her heart. He stood there for a while and walked away again. Minutes passed. Joe looked in her direction again. She turned away from him and began to walk, looking down. Joe went to her, his head at her back. Together, they walked around the pen, making patterns. He was glued to her.

"I am dying to know what was happening in there!" I exclaimed when Katie exited the round pen. She explained that her heart's desire was to go on an adventure with Joe. Once inside the pen, though, her head filled with limiting beliefs. She couldn't go on an adventure, they were in this enclosed space, she thought. It was ridiculous to think she could do that, the voice in her head continued. Then, she closed her eyes and returned to her heart space. That was the moment Joe walked to her, aligning his heart with her's. After he walked away, she realized that circumstances in life are never going to be perfect. There will always be "limitations" if you believe they exist. Somehow, she had to find a way to meet her heart's desire no matter what was happening in life.

With that in mind, she chose to change her energy. She decided to imagine the round pen was a beautiful forest she wanted to explore. Once her mindset, actions and energy became congruent with her desire, Joe chose to go with her on that adventure.

Lessons

1. "...all energy has a frequency and all frequency carries information."--Joe Dispenza. We can choose the information we want to transmit by changing our thoughts and emotions which comprise our energy.

Zen Koan

Long ago there lived a famous wrestler whose name meant "Great Waves." He was massively strong and knew the art of wrestling. In private bouts he defeated even his teacher, yet in public was so bashful that even his students threw him down.

Troubled, the wrestler decided to visit a Zen temple for help. There, a wise teacher advised him.

"Great Waves is your name," said the teacher. "So spend to-night in the temple. Imagine that you are water. You are no longer a wrestler who is afraid. You are those powerful waves sweeping over everything in sight. Do this and you will never again be defeated."

The teacher left. The wrestler sat still, trying to imagine himself as water. His mind wandered but soon he began to feel more and more like moving waves. As night advanced the waves grew taller and taller. They swept away the flowers and rushed over the statues. Before dawn the temple was nothing but the tide of a vast ocean.

In the morning the teacher found the wrestler in meditation with a slight smile on his face. He patted the man's shoulder. "Now nothing can disturb you," he said. "You are those waves. You will sweep everything before you."

The same day the wrestler entered and won a prestigious tournament, and was never defeated again.

Lessons

1. "Sometimes the most challenging opponents we face live inside of us. When we look with honesty inside our own hearts, that is where we find the self-belief we seek."--Buddha Groove

2. "Everything changes when you start to emit your own frequency, rather than absorbing the frequencies around you, when you start imprinting your intent on the universe rather than receiving an imprint from existence." -- Barbara Marciniak

We are intimately connected to all beings. Consider that whatever energy is brought to an interaction changes the outcomes whether we are conscious of it or not. What happens when our energy is controlled by outside forces?

When we allow circumstances to dictate our inner states, it is easy to fall prey to negative, survival emotions like fear, anger, frustration or any limiting beliefs we carry. The physiological response is one of survival. Our heart rate increases, our pupils dilate, we leave the thinking part of our brain and prepare for fight, flight or freeze. Stress hormones flood the body and, if this state becomes chronic, we become addicted to these chemicals, magnetically attracting negative events to satisfy a chemical need. Negative energy can be felt by all sentient beings. We have all had the experience of walking into a room and hitting a wall of residual anger. Even if the people in the room act as if all is well, the energy is undeniable.

By becoming aware of our thoughts and emotions, we can choose with intention the energy we want to bring to any situation. According to the Heart Math Institute, the physiological response to feelings of awe, gratitude, love and joy creates coherence between brain activity and heart rate, releasing a cascade of feel good hormones. The Law of Attraction states that like energy attracts like energy, so it follows that the positive energy you emit will attract positive energy in return. The following activities provide you the opportunity to feel the energetic presence and intention of your horse, to communicate beyond words and to experience your body as an energetic sensory device.

Benefits of Energetic awareness
1. Become aware of yourself as both the energy and the sensing instrument you are
2. Attune to subtle energetic sensations
3. Sense your body's messages
4. Increase curiosity through finding comfort in the unknown

Activities
1. The Energetic Alignment of Play
When was the last time you played? Think of the energy needed for the spirit of play. Playfulness is a soup of intention, curiosity, your heart's desire, imagination and action, all in a context that is relaxed and fun. Have a play session with your horse. In a space where you feel safe, spend time breathing into and out of your heart. Open your heart by summoning an elevated emotion. Invite your 5 year old self to express her/himself. Send that energy into the heart field of your horse, inviting him to join you in play. Get creative with toys, musical instruments...Let your imagination soar!

2. Fully Alive
Think of a time in your life when you felt fully, exuberantly alive. With your eyes closed, go to that time. Where were you? What were you doing? Feel the energy of that moment. Every cell in

your body was inspired, everything was in technicolor. What did you see? What did you smell? How did you feel? What was the look on your face? Staying in that moment, go into your heart. Write down 5 adjectives that describe the essence of your experience. These words represent your timeless essence. For you, they mean, "I am really, fully alive!" This is the person your horse wants to know.

3. Focal not Vocal

Play with focus. Set an intention for your horse to move in a specific way, perhaps stepping under with her hind left leg. Maintain a steady focus on the area of his body until she responds to your focus. The more you practice focus, the stronger your intention will become. This can be done in the saddle as well. Simply visualize any movement you wish, focusing on the part of the horse's body that will need to move first. Where you place your attention is where you place your energy. Before long, you will be communicating telepathically.

4. Bodywork

Doing bodywork on your horse will make you feel grounded and will work that focus muscle. While doing this, you must be present, aware and mindful. Bodywork cultivates a sense of deep connection, builds trust and enhances your intuition. Begin at your horse's poll with your fingertips about an inch away from your horse's hair. Glide your hand along the topline without touching. Pay close attention to your horse's subtle responses. They may include blinking, yawning, shaking. When your horse responds, stop at that spot until there is a release in the form of an exhale or a yawn. Then, continue along his back to the top of his tail. Notice how you are sending an energy current through the space gap between your fingertips and the horse. Learn some massage techniques for your horse. Doing bodywork on your horse creates a healing, calming heart connection as your body and your horse's body rest in a resonant field.

EQUANIMITY
Chapter VII

"There's a huge amount of freedom that comes to you when you take nothing personally."--Miguel Ruiz

Katie and Joe
"For once, while on the mounting block, instead of feeling anxiety, I felt a centered stillness and a relaxed awareness. Now, although I know Joe's behavior was due to my energy, I am certain it is not personal."

To explore equanimity, the group chose an activity that challenges them with their horses. For Katie, that anxiety inducing activity was standing on the mounting block, trying to mount Joe while he danced around. To get on her horse, Katie would, as quickly as possible, get a foot in a stirrup and swing her other leg over whenever he offered her two seconds. Just standing on the mounting block, though, the anticipation caused her to feel frustration and anxiety. This caused an increase in her heart rate, an elevation in her blood pressure and caused her breathing to become rapid and shallow. Joe's response was to nervously dance around. Why? Because Katie, at this point, had become a hungry predator who wanted to be on his back. Joe had reason to be nervous.

Before working with their horses, we practiced equanimity ahead of the experience. Practicing what you want to feel in your body, ahead of the event, sets you up for greater success. We intentionally activated the attitudes of our inner sage, including curiosity, innovation, confidence and fearlessness.

First, we explored what curiosity feels like in the body. What is the expression on your face when you are curious? What is your body posture? How do you hold your head? The ladies then "posed" in a stance that represented curiosity. In that pose, we discussed what felt possible. Next, we imagined innovation in the body, noting how the expressions on the women's faces had changed along with the shifts in body posture. This was followed by summoning confidence. While imagining the attitude of confidence, they noticed what it felt like in their eyes, head, face, stomach and chest. Finally, we explored fear, differentiating between fear and vulnerability and discerning when our fears pretend to be logic. What would one's posture look like if you were capable of being and doing anything you wanted? As they shifted their postures, they felt their spines grounded deep into the Earth.

Combining all of the attitudes of a Superhero, they searched inside their bodies to discover where their inner superhero lives. They placed a hand on that part of their bodies and breathed into it, anchoring it to help them remember. This is a sacred space between the doer of actions, the thinker of thoughts and the feeler of feelings. Your superhero is your wise observer. This is where equanimity lives, making you the steady ship in the storm, the person your horse can count on, can trust and depend upon.

In the arena with Joe, Katie stood on the mounting block. She took the time to become present. She released any attachment to the outcome and became absolutely clear in wanting all of Joe's feet to stay in one place. Knowing the affect her energy had on him, she summoned the emotion of Joy into her heart. She stood there, taking deep breaths, standing in the stance of her superhero self, relaxing into her heart. For his part, Joe was, at first hesitant, nervous. In his mind, why would this time be any different from the others? She ignored his movements while one hand held the reins and the other was placed on her solar plexus. After a couple of minutes, Joe stood quietly. Basking in her energy of joy, confidence and relaxed curiosity, he lowered his head. He yawned one of those big yawns, his tongue flopping out to either side of his mouth. When she felt ready, Katie put her foot in the stirrup, she breathed deeply and then swung her leg over, gently lowering herself into the saddle. Joe stood quietly and she patted him all over his neck, leaning over and touching her face to his mane.

Lessons

1. "To cultivate equanimity, we practice catching ourselves when we feel attraction or aversion, before it hardens into grasping or negativity. "--Pema Chodron
2. "The best way to overcome fear is to face, with equanimity, the situation of which one is afraid."--B.K.S. Iyengar

Zen koan

During the countryside wars, a general swept from town to town, conquering each place with ease. In one particular town, the general discovered that everyone had fled just before his arm arrived--everyone except the Zen master.

Curious about what sort of man this was, the general visited the temple himself. Inside, the Zen master remained still, and refused to bow or even move out of the general's way. When it was clear the Zen master would not defer to the general's power, he became furious.

"Fool!" he shouted, as he drew his weapon, "Don't you see you are standing before a man who would run through you without blinking an eye?"

The Zen master responded with absolute calm.

"And don't you see that you are standing before a man who could be run through without blinking an eye?"

Humbled by the Zen master's resolve, the general regrouped his forces and returned from where they had come.

Lessons
1. "A modern definition of equanimity: cool. This refers to one whose mind remains stable and calm in all situations."--Allan Lokos
2. "There is never any need to get worked up or to trouble your soul about things you cannot control. These things are not asking to be judged by you. Leave them alone."--Marcus Aurelius

Equanimity is defined as "Neither a thought nor an emotion, it is rather the steady conscious realization of reality's transience. It is the ground for wisdom and freedom and the protector of compassion and love...The Buddha described a mind filled with equanimity as 'abundant, exalted, immeasurable, without hostility and without ill-will'."--Gil Fronsdal, Insight Meditation Center. How can one remain even tempered and calm in difficult situations?

Equanimity is something to be cultivated with baby steps, the ultimate being a psychological state that is unfazed by experience, emotion or pain. The baby steps are the aesthetic principles our horses teach us. Through mindfulness, we remain connected and compassionate with things as they are. Through clear awareness, we learn to transform challenges into lessons as we remain open, curious and present to the situation. These practices lead us to no longer judge things as "wrong" when they are simply different. When we strive towards equanimity, we release the illusion that we can control or manipulate circumstances to fit our desires.

Lessons
1. Shedding illusions is the key to a life of tranquility.
2. The only thing in life we have control over is our response to all situations
3. Life is an ever changing river. Striving towards equanimity prepares you to relate to life moment to moment.

Benefits of Equanimity
1. Wisdom and peace become your natural state
2. Increased emotional intelligence allows you to respond in a composed, compassionate manner, remaining balanced during difficult situations
3. Creative solutions come to you effortlessly through your open heart and mind
4. Decreased suffering since nothing is taken per-

sonally

5. You become the conscious leader your horse can look to whenever he feels insecure

Activities

1. The 7 C's of Well Being

- **Courage**--the ability to do something dangerous, or that puts you in a vulnerable position. People low on courage have feelings of powerlessness, overwhelm and often feel "stuck" in relationships or jobs.

- **Creativity**--the ability to entertain new things or new ideas, to use your imagination, to express curiosity and to play. People low on creativity feel uninspired and unproductive.

- **Clarity**--the ability to set intentions and goals, take action, be motivated, find meaning and purpose. People low on clarity are negative, frustrated, have no focus or feel they are "spinning in circles".

- **Calm-** the ability to maintain a quiet, peaceful state. People low on calmness experience overwhelm, anxiety, stormy conditions or they may be flat and dissociated.

- **Compassion--**the ability to have a high self worth, self compassion and forgiveness. People low on compassion are hyper critical of themselves, do not believe they can achieve goals and are often pessimistic.

- **Congruence-**the ability to be in agreement or harmony and act in accordance with your dreams, desires, beliefs, values, mission and goals. People low on congruence do things out of a sense of "duty". Their body language does not match their words.

- **Connection-**the ability to connect to one's feelings and higher self/ personal source for guidance, to feel a sense of oneness with other sentient beings. People low on connection tend to push others away, avoid responsibility for their own feelings and often experience resentment.

Think of a situation in life. Assign a rating for each C on a scale of 1-5. When you score low, using courage as an example, ask yourself, "what is 'courage' for me?"
"What might be an experience with my horse that represents 'courage' for me?" Next, create an interaction with your horse that represents every C you assigned a low score.

2. The Sculpture
Using the same C's you assigned a low score to, shape your body into a sculpture that represents the low C. In that position, ask yourself, "What is possible in this shape? What feels hard or impossible? What emotions or stories come up for me in this shape?" If possible, have a friend take a photo of you in that position so you can look at it afterwards. Next, name the quality you want to cultivate. Shape your body this time to represent the desired quality. Ask yourself the above questions in your new shape. This activity is great to do with your horses present. Take note of their response to each of your sculptures.

3. List your Illusions
Make a list of all of the things you would like to change about your horse, life, relationships, etc...For each one, ask yourself if there is something you can do about it. If so, there is no problem. If you cannot do anything about it,

then, also, there is no problem. For each illusion you can do something about, write a plan for what you will do. For those you cannot change, list strategies for finding peace.

TRANQUILITY AND SERENITY
Chapter VIII

"The beauty of Zen is found in simplicity and tranquility, in a sense of the all-embracing harmony of things."--Thich Thien-An

Katie and Joe
"Over the course of the weekend, I was able to move from a place of frustration and fear to one of implicit trust and allowance of the gifts Joe wants to offer me. Instead of my 'therapy', I know him now as my teacher, speaking through my heart, guiding me to serenity."

I save Tranquility, the last principle of enlightenment for the final activity of the workshop. All of the principles deepen and strengthen your relationship with your horse but this last one connects you in a way that will transform your horse's experience with you, making him or her look to you for comfort and safety, building a deeper level of trust. As sentient beings, mammals naturally co-regulate their nervous systems with each other. When you are in the presence of another who is calm, your body will become calm just as when you are in the presence of chaos, your body will certainly feel the chaos. So often, when we are with our horses, we have an agenda. There is grooming, saddling, schooling, washing...much of which is done without the person being fully present with the horse. How often do you set out with the intention to experience tranquility with your horse?

For the final activity of the workshop, the group chose a

guided meditation from several options. With the horses loose in the arena, the women sat on the ground or in chairs, depending on where they felt the most comfortable. During the meditation, I guided them to bring awareness to each of their senses, paying exquisite attention to the experiences of each one. Next, they summoned the child in them-the beautiful essence free from all stories. As we continued in meditation, the horses began gathering around. Some stood in front of their partners, heads lowered, eyes half open. Loud noises of contentment spread around the circle, horses exhaling, lips flapping, snot flying. Three of the horses, including Joe, began pawing the ground, readying it as a bed. They lowered themselves down with deep exhalations. Joe rolled, his big belly facing the sky before stretching his legs out to rest. He rubbed the side of his face in the sand and settled into stillness. He was not far from Katie.

Ending the meditation and opening their eyes, the women sat in peace and wondered at the sights surrounding them. The horses were in complete relaxation with them. All sounds had gone quiet as if nature herself was conspiring to add to the tranquility. The beauty of the scene brought tears to our eyes. We stayed like this for a very long while, until some of the horses started to slowly move about. Human and horse bodies alike were heavy with relaxation. The women began to drag themselves into hugs with the other women and with the horses. Heads were buried in big, strong necks, tears of joy were streaming down cheeks.

Joe aligned his heart with Katie's, his head over her neck and her face pressed into his shoulder. She breathed in his scent and said she had never felt so close to him as at that moment.

Zen koan

Open Your Own Treasure House. Daiju visited the master Baso in China.

Baso asked: "What do you seek?"

"Enlightenment," replied Daiju.

"You have your own treasure house. Why do you search outside?" Baso asked.

Daiju inquired: "Where is my treasure house?"

Baso answered: "What you are asking is your treasure house."

Daiju was enlightened! Ever after he urged his friends: "Open your own treasure house and use those treasures."

Lessons

1. Tranquility comes when you, "Realize that your soul has all of the answers that you seek."--The Ancient Ones
2. "Each person possesses a precious inner treasure of infinite worth."--Daisaku Ikeda

"Eventually you have to move from looking and go into feeling, realizing that feeling is a sense, too. Not the touch of the fingers, but the touch of the heart. This kind of touch has another dimension, deeper than that possessed by fingers."--The Secret Teachings of Plants: The Intelligence of the Heart in the Direct Perception of Nature, by Stephen Harrod Buhner.

Tranquility is found in the touch of the heart. It flows naturally from horses grazing silently in a verdant field. They model deep contentment that comes from inner guidance and the peaceful interconnection of the herd, where all hearts beat as one in coherence.

The following activities are designed to bring your heart into coherence where tranquility is found. When you join the horses in their natural state, they will respond in seemingly unusual ways. They might lay down, stand over you licking and chewing and yawning, or relax into a deep sleep. Relax your mind and allow your inner treasure to shine in the knowledge that all is exactly as you've designed it. Rest here, sharing peace and serenity with your horse. If tears want to come, let them.

Lessons

1. "Wordless, spirit speaks. In silence, we hear all answers."--Zen proverb
2. "Serenity is the tranquil balance of heart and mind."--Harold W. Becker

Benefits of Tranquility

1. Quality of life increases dramatically when you devote time to peace and tranquility each day
2. Trust and respect deepen when your horse can count on you to be tranquil and equanimous
3. Every moment gives you the option of choosing peace over stress

Activities

1. Conversations with horse

Sit with your horse in nature. Take time to stop, breath deeply, gaze at your horse. Notice how it feels. Notice each of your senses individually.

Imagine you are experiencing life as your horse does in that moment. Allow all sounds to move through you as the waves they are. Look at your horse as if your very sight is a warm embrace. Ask your horse what he would like for you to know. Listen with your heart.

2. Qi gong

Learn a Qi Gong routine to practice in the pasture. My horse, Bo, loves to participate. He will copy my movements, in his own way, raising his head high up in the air then lowering it to the ground, moving from side to side. He usually ends by pawing the ground and laying down.

3. Yoga

Take your yoga mat to the barn. Achieve higher consciousness and body flexibility by practicing in the presence of your horse.

4. Mandala

A mandala is a mystic symbol of the universe. Traditionally, it is a circle in a square which includes images of deities and is used as a focus in meditation. Design one with symbols of your relationship with your horse and your life together.

5. Sit and Breathe

"Breeze blowing wind chimes, the feel of sun on your face. Sit quietly--Be."--Buddha. Cultivate tranquility while relieving anxiety and stress with breath work. There are many intentional breathing techniques. A simple one is to inhale to

the count of 4, allowing your ribs to expand outward. Hold your breath for 7 counts. Exhale for
the count of 8 while also stretching your spine
upwards. Repeat this breath while simultaneously
noticing all of your senses.

CONCLUSION

While you may not be interested in the commitment required to be a Zen monk, the benefits of becoming more Zen greatly impact our quality of life and relationships. It gives us a clear path to greater connection with our horses and loved ones. When we learn to nourish our minds and bodies, we have no choice but to treat others with more compassion, love and kindness.

It is said that horses mirror us. Their alert, deep attunement to our psychophysiological states is reflected in their behavior when they are in our presence. They "mirror" us by behaving as an outward reflection of our inner states. As we become more aware of how our energetic states affect our horses and all of those around us, we can make choices in how we want to feel and set intentions for the information we want to convey. With this knowledge, we must accept full responsibility for the outcomes of all of our interactions. Though we cannot control outside events, we can choose the ways in which we allow them to sway us and make an intentional choice in how to respond. The following 12 essential rules to live like a Zen monk will provide you the skills to slow time, live in peace and greatly enhance the quality of your life. "Intention is the seed that creates our future."--Buddhist proverb.

1. When you drink tea, drink tea. If you have ever tried to rush and multi-task with a horse, you know the fruitlessness of this endeavor. Do one thing at a time.
2. Do it slowly and deliberately, being present

and alert. Groom your horse with the intention of giving him pleasure. This is an intimate time with your equine partner. If your mind begins to wander, return to your task and be there with him in connection.

3. Do it completely. Do not rush on to other tasks until you've completed the first one.

4. Do less.

5. Put space between things. Before moving to the next task, take a moment to rest and relish the pause.

6. Develop rituals. Rituals cultivate trust with our horses. When we imbue actions with purpose, every experience is enriched.

7. Designate time for certain things. Horses appreciate patterns. By developing rituals and patterns, our horses know what to expect next and trust is built through that knowledge.

8. Devote time to sitting. When I sit in the pasture with my horses, it gives them an opportunity to explore me and to enjoy tranquility with me, free from expectations.

9. Smile and serve others. By caring for our horses, we are nurturing ourselves. Show your gratitude for the privilege of being in the presence of your horse.

10. Make cleaning and cooking and grooming a meditation. Breathe, feel, sense, connect.

11. Think about what is necessary in the moment. You will find that, in presence, you have everything you need.

12. Live simply, make room for the essentials.

> Life is only as complicated as we make it.
> Notice how your horse models simplicity
> for you. Follow his lead.

I will end this book with a prayer of my own to all of you
and your horses,

May you find joy in the presence of your horse
May you become mindful, able to hear, in the silence, your
horse's wisdom
May you find clarity in the mystery of the questions and
know that the answers live in your heart
May you rejoice in your true nature and celebrate the glorious, unique nature of your horse
May you attune to the subtle energies, trusting your intuition so that you may cultivate trust in yourself
May you find peace in your life and your relationships
May you join your horse in equanimity, serenity and grace
as he guides you on the Buddhist path.

Namaste.

ABOUT THE AUTHOR

Michelle Hefner

Michelle Hefner is an author and coach who invites clients out of the box and into the arena of possibilities. In her coaching practice, she incorporates the ancient arts of alchemy, tapestry weaving and exploration in coaching individuals, teams and leaders who are ready to create and transform with intention. She assists clients in turning common ideas into rare and precious concrete manifestations, supports them in weaving new tapestries from the threads of their lives and holds momentum for those charting new courses, turning questions into exciting, future oriented challenges.

As a certified equine assisted coach, as well, her passion is in deepening the bonds of trust between people and their horses through her weekend Equinelightenment retreat.